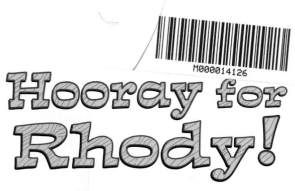

Hooray for Rhody!

By Marcia Vaughan
Illustrated by Mary O'Keefe Young

CELEBRATION PRESS
Pearson Learning Group

Contents

♪♫ Chapter 1 ♏

Bound for Oregon

My name is Rhoda May Baker, but everybody calls me Rhody. I was born in Missouri where my papa, Jack Baker, grew up. He was the son of a shopkeeper. My mama, Sarah, was raised on a dairy farm nearby. I'm the oldest in my family. My little brother Jasper is seven, and Clara is three. We all have the same flaming red hair as Mama and the same sea-green eyes as Papa.

My folks decided to move to the Oregon Territory because the land was free for the taking. Of course you still had to clear the trees, build a house, and farm the land, but after that, it was all yours. When you did that, it was called a land claim.

When I was nine, our neighbors, Mr. and Mrs. Ostram, left for the Oregon Territory. Soon they wrote to say how good the land there was for farming.

"We could start our own homestead there," Papa had said, and Mama agreed.

There were 50 wagons in our train as we pulled out of Independence, Missouri, on April 25, 1847. Each wagon was pulled by horses or teams of big, strong oxen. Our wagon looked mighty fine at the beginning of the trip. We'd painted it sky blue with red wheels. It had a new canvas top as white as the clouds above.

Our wagon was packed full with food, tools, a tent, bedding, clothes, a plow, and Mama's rocking chair. My, how Mama loved that chair! It had roses carved all over it and had been in her family for a very long time. She wouldn't agree to go until Papa promised he'd take it.

What I remember most about our trip were the endless days of walking. I also recall the dust rising up from every wagon. It coated me in dirty grit from my bonnet to my boots.

✎ Chapter 2 ✑
Our New Home

Nearly six months had passed by the time we reached the Willamette Valley. It was autumn, and there was barely a lick of paint left on our battered old wagon. That wagon had brought us all the way across the prairie, the rivers, and the mountains to our new home.

We'd been on our claim three days when neighbors came calling. Our old friends Mr. and Mrs. Ostram and a nearby family, the McGees, came to see us.

Mr. Ostram and Mr. McGee offered to help Papa clear the land and build the cabin. Mrs. Ostram gave us a rooster and six brown hens. She also gave us seeds for the garden we'd plant in the spring. Mrs. McGee had baked us a fresh fruit pie. I hadn't tasted a pie like that in months!

The next morning, under a gray sky, work on the cabin began. Jasper and I helped by marking the tallest, straightest trees in the forest so the men knew which to cut down.

Then Papa and the men chopped down the trees and cut them into logs. The logs were notched at each end and stacked on top of each other in a large square. Windows and a door were cut.

Next the plank roof was topped with cedar shingles. The floor of the cabin was made from split logs. The logs were so fresh that the sap still oozed from them.

To keep the wind out, we learned how to fill the cracks between the logs. We used a mixture of mud, moss, and straw. "This is called chinking," Mama said. It was messy work, but also fun. Clara got more mud on herself than she did on the wall.

Oh, were we ever happy to move into our new home! We were all tired of living in that cold, cramped wagon. To us the cabin seemed as big and as fancy as a castle.

"Old Man Winter can blow all he wants now. We'll be snug and safe in this fine cabin!" Mama declared as she rocked Clara.

"How about a tall tale?" Papa asked.

"Yes, Papa!" Jasper and I cried.

"Well," Papa said, "have you heard the one about Paul Bunyan and his big blue ox, Babe?" Papa had told the story to us many times before, but it seemed even better hearing it in our snug, new cabin.

The cold months passed and spring came creeping in. Papa hitched up our horse Dandy to plow a vegetable garden on one side of the cabin. We all helped plant the seeds our neighbors had given us for tomatoes, beans, potatoes, turnips, and squash.

The next day Papa plowed a larger field on the other side of the cabin. As he unpacked the corn seed, he yelped.

"Mice have eaten more than half of it," he said angrily, "and what's left looks mighty soggy."

"Oh, no!" Mama cried. "It got wet?"

Papa nodded grimly. "All we can do now is plant it and hope it grows. I don't know what we'll use for money if there is no corn to sell."

Mama put her hand on Papa's arm. "Don't worry, Jack. We'll think of something."

✌ Chapter 3 ✍

Mama's Rocking Chair

When Mrs. McGee stopped in, we heard news about a neighbor. "Ned Riley's going to California to get married," she told Mama. "He's selling his sheep and cow. If you're interested, I'll tell him to come by."

"We don't have sheep, and we sure could use another cow," Mama said.

The next afternoon Ned Riley knocked on our door. Mama told us kids to go outside so they could talk. When Mr. Riley came out, he put Mama's rocking chair into his wagon and drove off whistling.

Mama came out wiping her eyes.

"Why did he take your chair?" Jasper asked in surprise.

"I traded it for a milk cow and ten sheep, Jasper," Mama told us.

"But, Mama, you loved that chair," I said.

"Indeed I did, Rhody," she said, "but a rocking chair doesn't give milk or grow wool. Mr. Riley plans to give that chair to his bride for a wedding present."

Early the next day Mr. Riley came back with a brown milk cow named Dixie. She was a little bony, but otherwise seemed to be in good shape. Mr. Riley also brought ten of the strangest-looking sheep I had ever seen.

The sheep did not have pure black wool or
pure white wool. Instead they had white wool
with big, black patches in it.

Last of all Mr. Riley took an old spinning
wheel out of his wagon. He told Mama he
was throwing it in for free.

"Why do the sheep have those funny black
patches?" I asked Jasper after Mr. Riley left.

"I don't know," he said with a shrug.

Mrs. Ostram knew. She put her hands on her hips and shook her head. "The spotted fleece is worth less than pure black or pure white fleece. And that cow looks awfully thin."

Mama didn't seem to mind. "Mr. Riley told me the truth about them, but we have good grazing here. That cow will fatten up. And one sheep is as good as another to me," she said. "We'll take good care of them. Their fleece could come in handy some day."

The sheep's wool was long. Shearing it was hard work, but we did it. We washed the wool in the creek. When it dried, we stored it up in the rafters of the cabin.

As spring stretched into summer, the vegetables in the garden grew and grew. Dixie fattened up and gave us buckets of milk. The sheep grew fine and fat and gave birth to four lambs. The only thing that wasn't doing well was Papa's corn.

ᔔ Chapter 4 ᔕ
Papa Looks for Gold

It was Mr. McGee who brought word of what had been discovered at Sutter's Mill in California.

"Gold!" he shouted as he galloped up on his big bay mare. "Jack, Sarah, they found gold! Miners are going to Sutter's Mill like bees to honey and they're getting rich as kings!" He jumped down. "Jack," he said, slapping Papa on the back, "I'm going, too! You're welcome to join me if you'd like."

Mama and Papa had a long talk that night. The poor corn crop meant we'd lack money to buy supplies for next winter. In the morning Papa told us he was going with Mr. McGee.

He hugged me and Jasper to him. "You help Mama take care of Clara and our farm."

"What about the corn crop?" I asked.

"There won't be much corn, I'm afraid," Papa said. "With luck I'll find some other yellow thing that will be worth even more!"

We missed Papa something awful. During the day I missed the sound of his happy whistle as he worked. During the evening I missed his stories by the fire. Most of all I missed his good-night hugs.

We all pitched in doing the work Papa usually did. We even finished digging the root cellar.

The weeks went by. Summer was at its fullest. The days were long and hot.

One afternoon black clouds piled up in the sky like mounds of black wool. That night a terrible storm blew in. Lightning flashed. Drumming thunder boomed in the sky. Rain pounded at the cabin like fists. Clara cried as the wild wind ripped shingles off the roof. Rain leaked in, making puddles on the floor.

The next morning Mama went outside and found a bigger problem. "Oh, no," she said. "The corn is ruined!"

Jasper, Clara, and I ran outside.

"It looks like Paul Bunyan walked in the corn field," Jasper said while I nodded sadly.

"Thank goodness the cabin protected the vegetable garden from the worst of the wind. Most of the vegetables are all right," Mama said. "I hope your Papa is having better luck in the gold fields."

✂ Chapter 5 ∿

Mama's Clever Idea

One day Mama had an idea. "Jasper, please get the ladder and fetch a bundle of wool. I'm going to knit a surprise to give to Papa when he comes home."

Mama taught us how to card and spin the wool. To card it, we'd put a handful of wool between two special wire combs. Combing the wool straightened it. Instead of a fluffy bundle, it was now long threads that could be spun together.

I loved using the spinning wheel. As it turned the wooden spindle, a notch on the tip of the spindle caught the pieces of wool and twisted them together into strands of yarn.

Later, while we snuggled under our blankets, Mama sat in her chair and knitted.

"Do you think your papa will like these?" she asked one day. Laughing, she held up a pair of black and white striped socks.

"Mama," I said, "those are the craziest socks I've ever seen! Papa will think they are dandy. Will you teach me how to knit?"

"Get all your chores done first," she said. Knitting was harder than it looked. First I made a long woolly scarf. Then, I made a cap. Both had those crazy stripes. While I did that, Mama knitted a pair of gloves.

Many weeks later we heard the sound of a horse's hooves and a happy whistle coming up the trail. "Jack!" shouted Mama.

"Papa!" Jasper and Clara and I shouted.

Swinging off his horse, Papa threw his arms around all of us at once. That hug felt good all the way down to my toes.

"Did you find gold, Papa?" I asked.

"No, I didn't," he said. "By the time we got there, the good claims had already been taken, but there's more than one way to get rich in the gold fields."

"What do you mean?" Mama asked.

ꙍ Chapter 6 ꙍ
Hooray for Rhody!

"There are thousands of miners out there," Papa said, "and they are desperate for supplies. If you've got something they need, you can sell it for top dollar. I saw onions selling for a dollar each. A barrel of flour sold for 40 dollars! Next spring we'll make our garden bigger. We can sell our squash and potatoes and turnips. Those vegetables won't spoil on the way to California. We need something to to sell in the winter, though," he added.

Suddenly Mama stood up. "Jack, I almost forgot. I made a surprise for your homecoming."

She placed a small parcel wrapped in a scrap of red cloth in his hands.

Papa unwrapped it. He held up the black and white striped socks. "Well, these are the wildest socks I've ever seen! They'll keep my feet jumping just wearing them!"

Mama beamed.

"There's more, Papa," I cried. I pulled the gloves, hat, and scarf I'd made out of the knitting basket.

Papa put them all on at once. He danced a jig around the room.

"I'll be warm as bug in a rug come winter with these!" he sang.

Scooping Clara up in his arms, he hopped from foot to foot around the cabin. Mama and Jasper and I laughed out loud.

I watched Papa leaping about in all his
striped finery. Suddenly an idea raced into
my mind like a runaway horse.

"Knitting!" I cried. I jumped up so fast that
my bench fell over. "In winter we could sell
our knitting to those miners!"

Papa stood as still as a snowman. "Rhody,
that is a great idea!" he said. "Those miners
will be cold during winter. I bet they'll buy
everything you can knit!"

He put Clara down. Then he swung me around the room in a wild dance.

"Hooray for Rhody!" Clara sang.

By day we flew through our chores as fast as we could. Then we all knitted like crazy. Papa learned how to use a pair of knitting needles pretty quickly, while I taught Jasper. Even Clara helped by winding the yarn into balls. Soon we had knitted lots and lots of socks, gloves, hats, and scarves.

Papa made a deal with a trader named Mr. Hawk. Mr. Hawk took supplies to the shopkeepers at the mining towns. He paid Papa one dollar for each hat, scarf, pair of socks, and pair of gloves.

"I can sell these knit goods for two dollars each to the shopkeepers," Mr. Hawk told us. "The shopkeepers will raise the price to three dollars for the miners. We will all make money."

Now Mama and Papa had enough money to buy cloth for warm winter clothes. They could also buy flour, sugar, coffee, tea, and other food items that we could not grow.

The next day Papa left for the store with a long list. The sun hung low in the sky when he returned. The wagon was filled with sacks and boxes. There was something big in the back.

"Oh, Jack, now what fool thing did you go and buy?" Mama said with a smile.

"See for yourself, Sarah," he replied.

Mama reached over the side of the wagon. She pulled off the blanket. "Oh, Jack, my rocking chair!" she cried with joy. "Where did you find it?"

"I met up with Mr. Riley down the road. He lost most of his money in California. He and his wife decided to move back to their land claim. He was happy to sell me back your chair at a fair price."

Mama hugged Papa so hard that I thought she'd squeeze the stuffing right out of him.

Jasper climbed up into the wagon. "Papa," what's in this big crate?"

"Apple tree seedlings," Papa said. "We're going to turn that corn patch into an apple orchard. This climate is just right for growing big, sweet, juicy apples!"

We'd done it. We'd come all the way to Oregon and found a way to stay. Hooray!